METHUEN PAIRED READING STORYBOOKS

My Mum's a Window Cleaner

Bill Gillham

Illustrated by Margaret Chamberlain

Methuen Children's Books

Some mums work in shops.

Some mums drive buses.

But my mum's a window cleaner.

You have to be careful
when you walk under her
ladder . . .

or you might get a shower!

And when she swings her
ladder round . . .

you duck!

Sometimes she cleans
windows very low down,

and sometimes she cleans
windows very high up.

But my mum's not scared!

One day there was a big fire.

My mum ran up her
ladder . . .

with her bucket full of water.

She rescued a baby with his bottle . . .

a fat man having a bath . . .

even an old lady with a parrot.

Everybody cheered!

And when the firemen
arrived . . .

they gave her a helmet!

My mum's got a bigger ladder now.

But she doesn't clean
windows any more.

She's a firelady instead!

How to pair read

1 Sit the child next to you, so that you can both see the book.

2 Tell the child you are *both* going to read the story *at the same time*. To begin with the child will be hesitant: adjust your speed so that you are reading almost simultaneously, *pointing to the words* as you go.

3 If the child makes a mistake, repeat the correct word but *keep going* so that fluency is maintained.

4 Gradually increase your speed once you and the child are reading together.

5 As the child becomes more confident, lower your voice and, progressively, try dropping out altogether.

6 If the child stumbles or gets stuck, give the correct word and continue 'pair-reading' to support fluency, dropping out again quite quickly.

7 Read the story *right through* once a day but not more than twice, so that it stays fresh.

8 After about 5-8 readings the child will usually be reading the book independently.

In its original form paired reading was first devised by Roger Morgan and Elizabeth Lyon, and described in a paper published in the Journal of Child Psychology and Psychiatry (1979).

First published in Great Britain 1988
by Methuen Children's Books Ltd, 11 New Fetter Lane, London EC4P 4EE
Text copyright © 1988 Bill Gillham
Illustrations copyright © 1988 Margaret Chamberlain
Printed in Hong Kong by Wing King Tong Co Ltd
ISBN 0 416 09732 4